Little Darlings

By Kelly Horton

Copyright 2018 Kelly Horton

ALL RIGHTS RESERVED

With the exception of those used in review's, the uncoloured or blank images herein, may not be reproduced, in whole or part by any means existing, other than for review.

The pages contained within are for personal use only. You may not distribute to or share uncoloured blank pages with any other colourists, in colouring groups, colouring group parties, via Email or message etc. to any other person, group, people or entity, and you may not upload blank or uncoloured pages to the internet without prior written permission of the artist and author Kelly Horton / The colouring Collective publications.

For any further details, including information on other books or colouring pages contact:

Kellyartistthorton@yahoo.com

For more colouring pages:

www.etsy.com/uk/Colourcollectiveshop

Join the Facebook Community at

The Colouring Collective

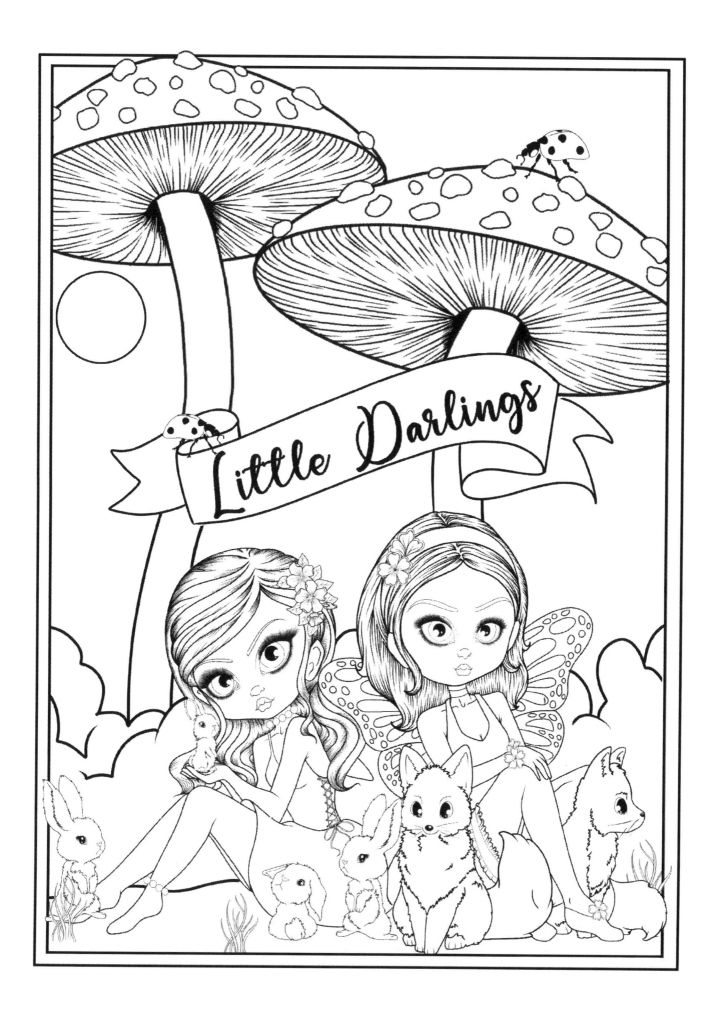

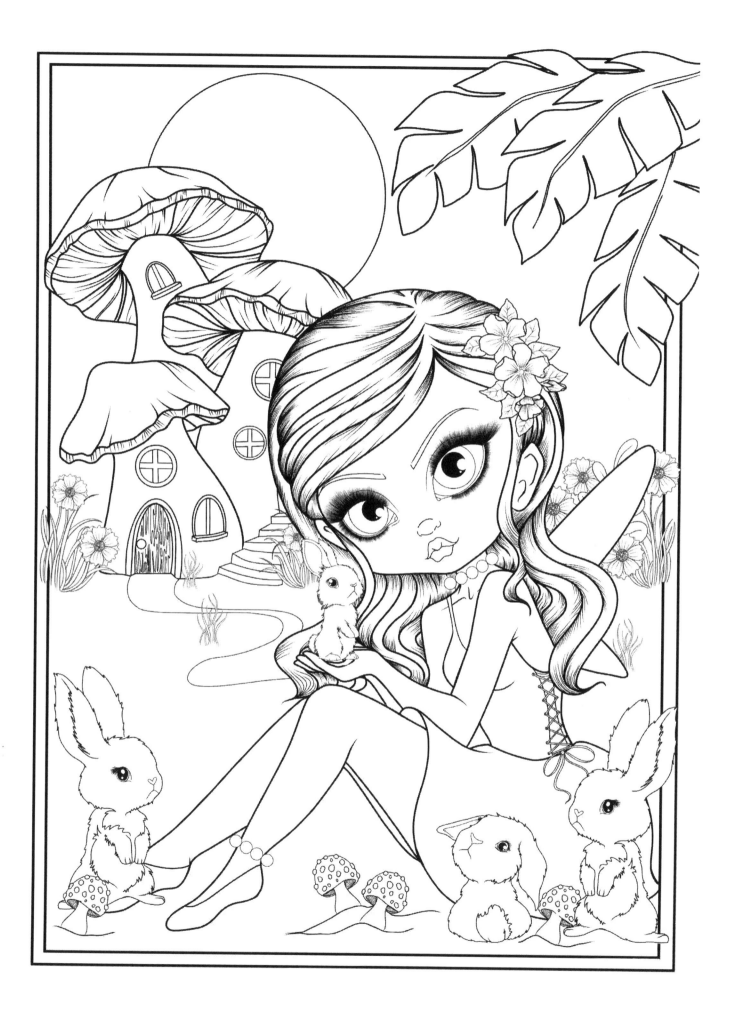

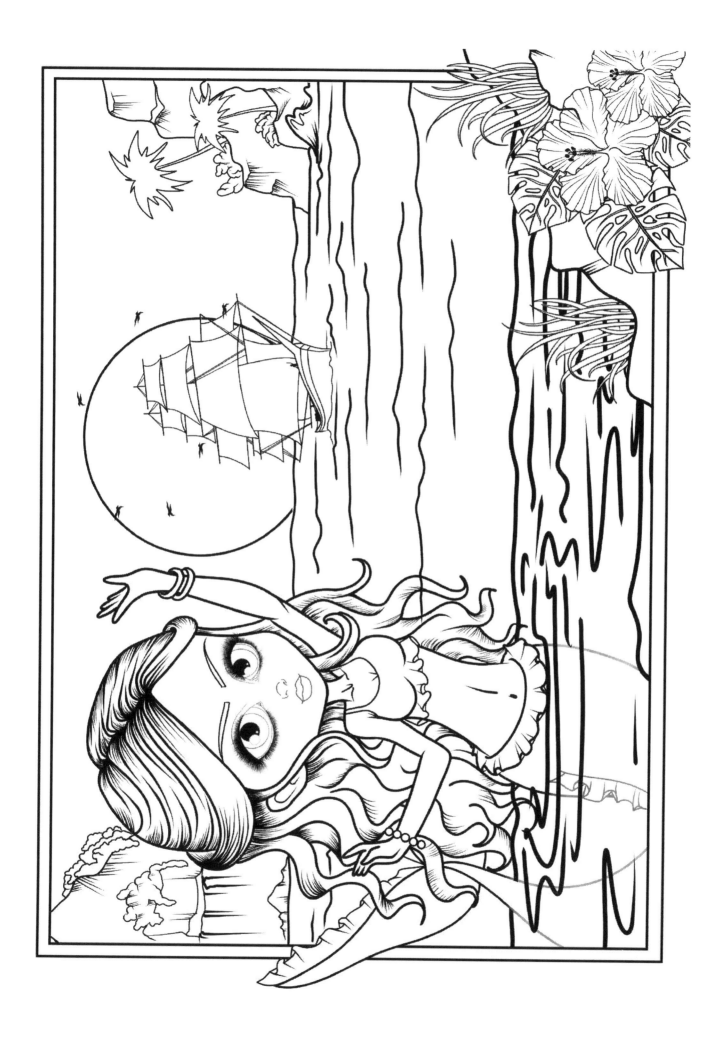

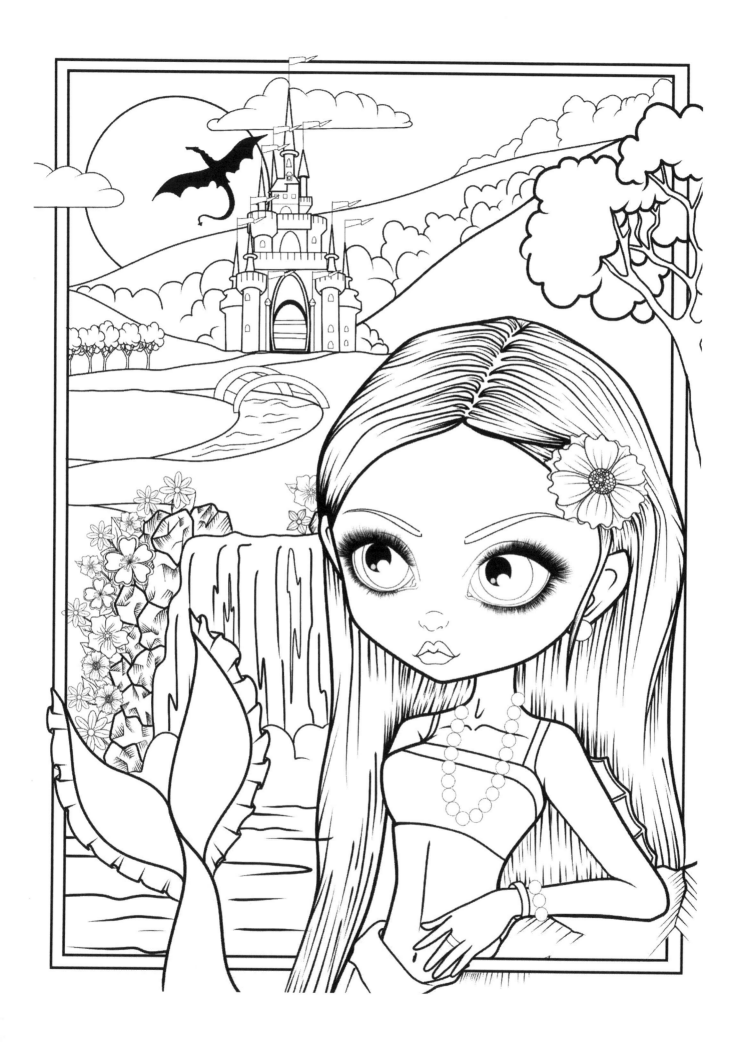

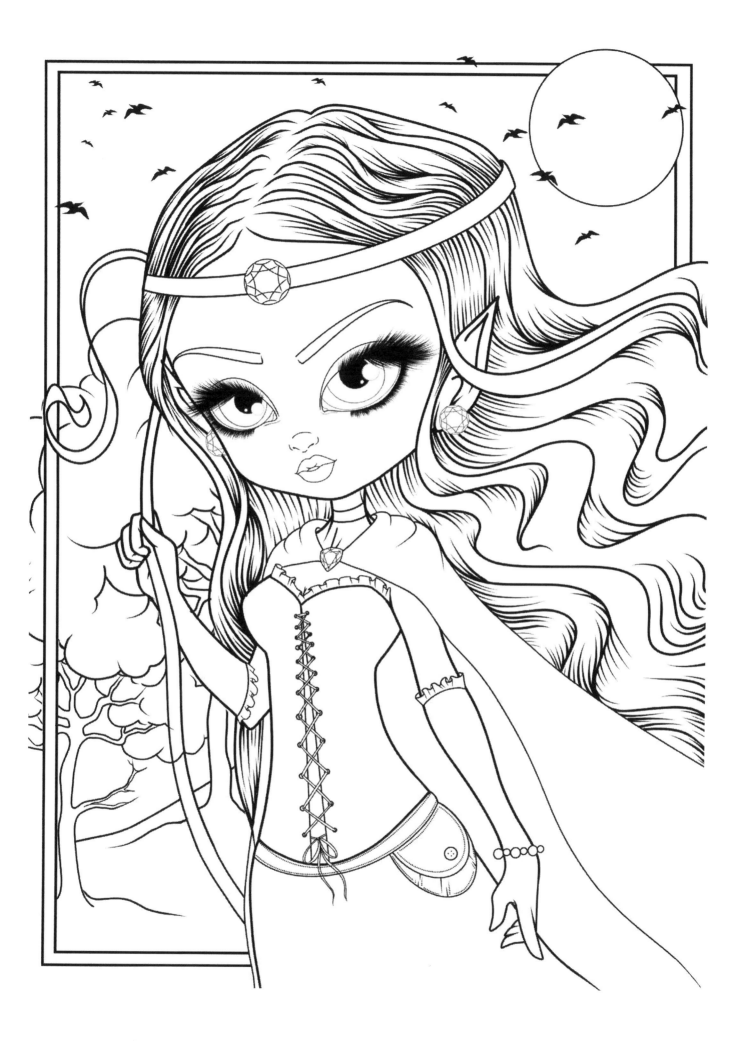

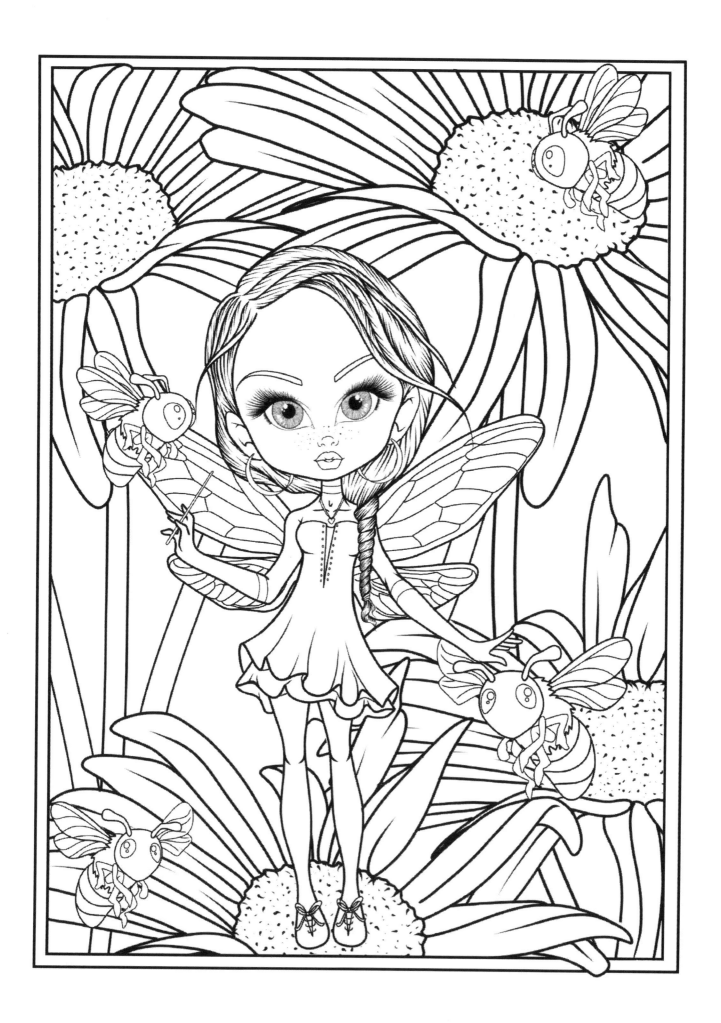

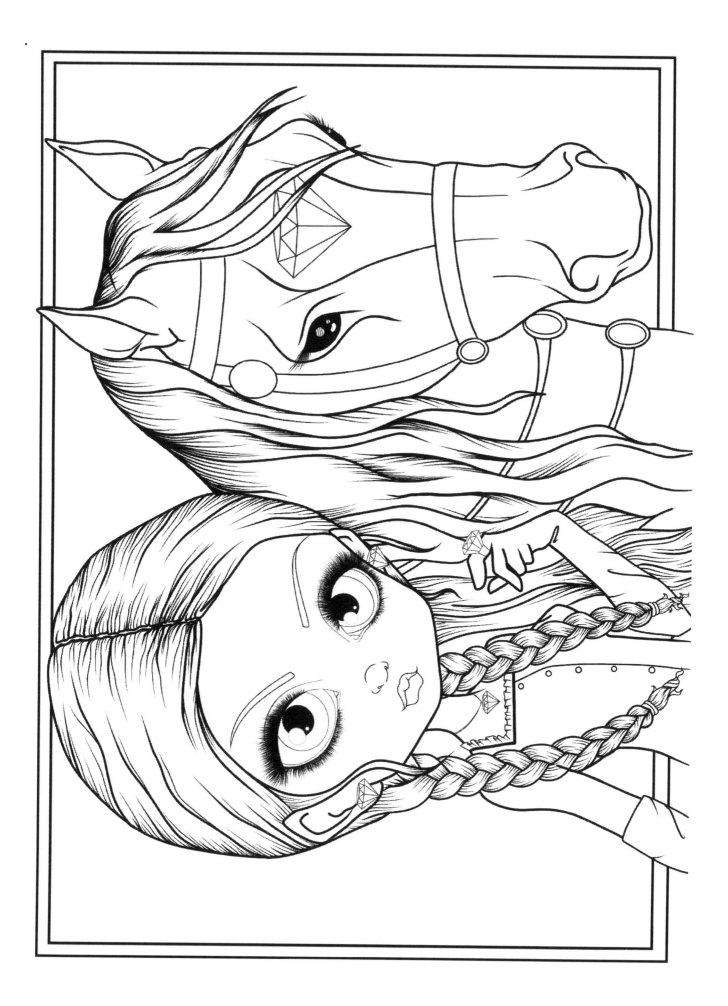

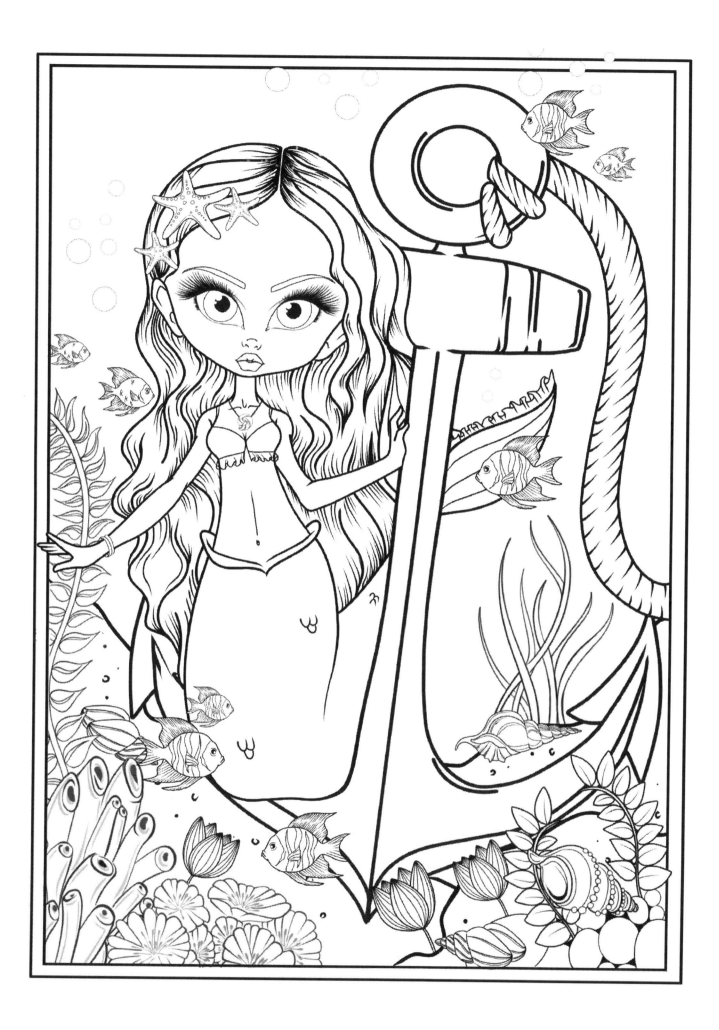

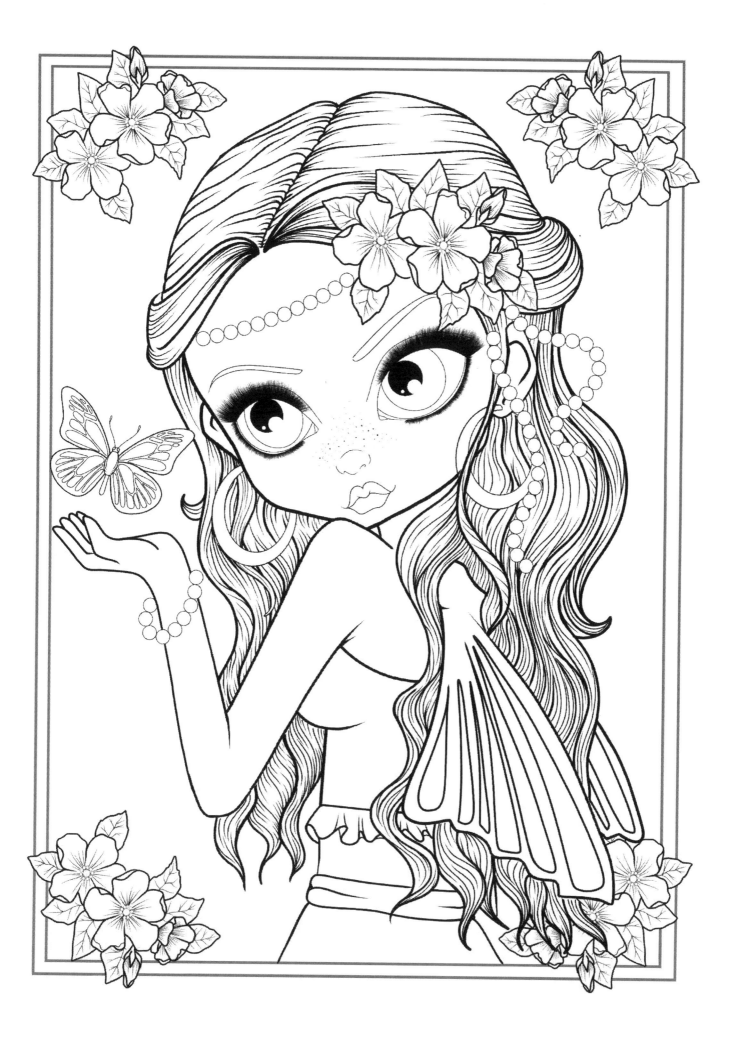

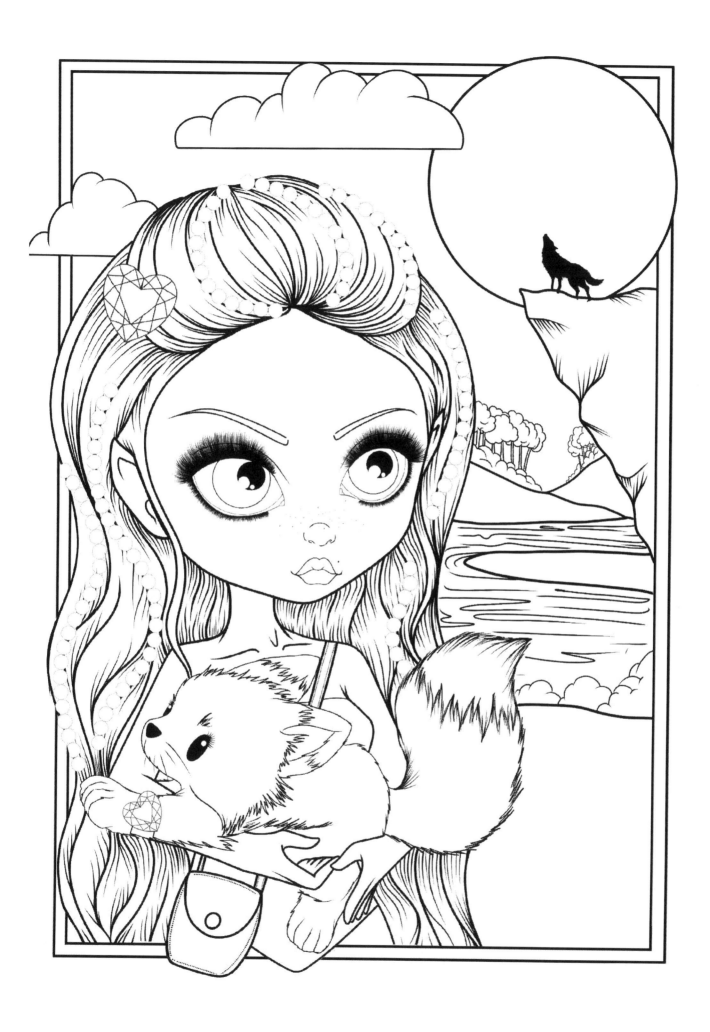

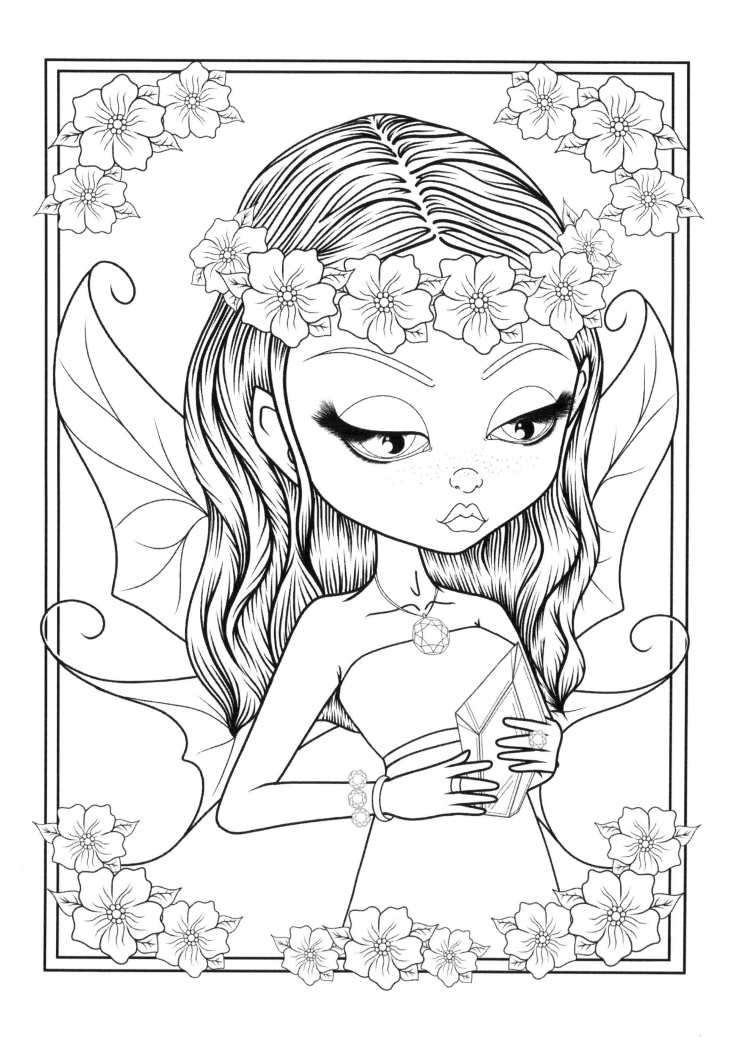

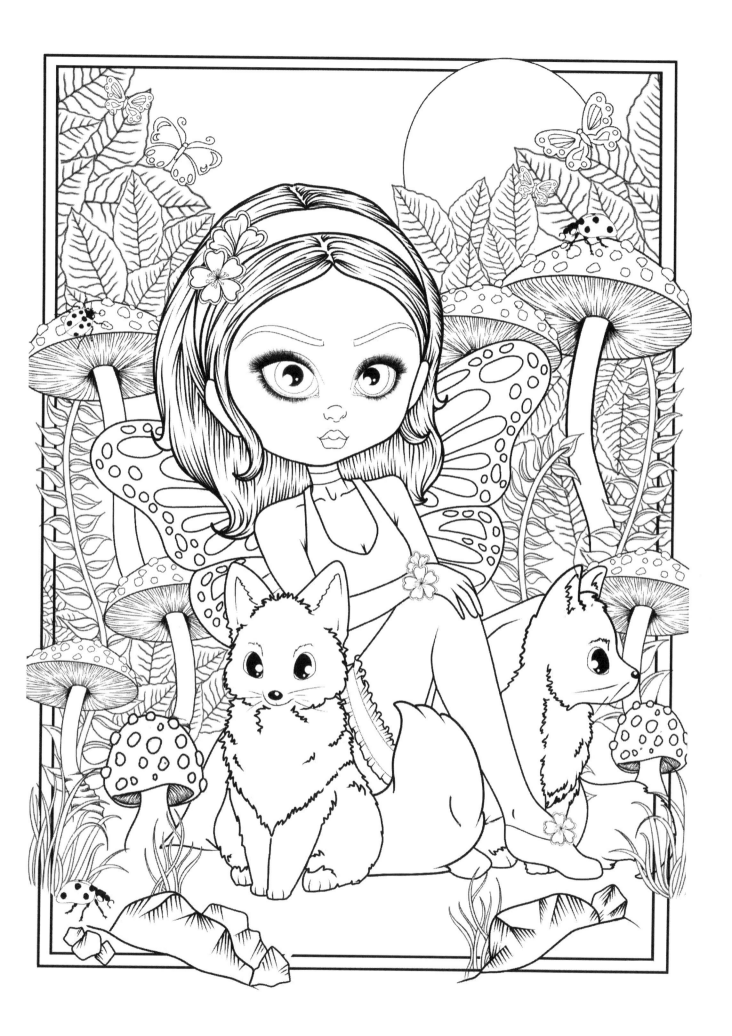

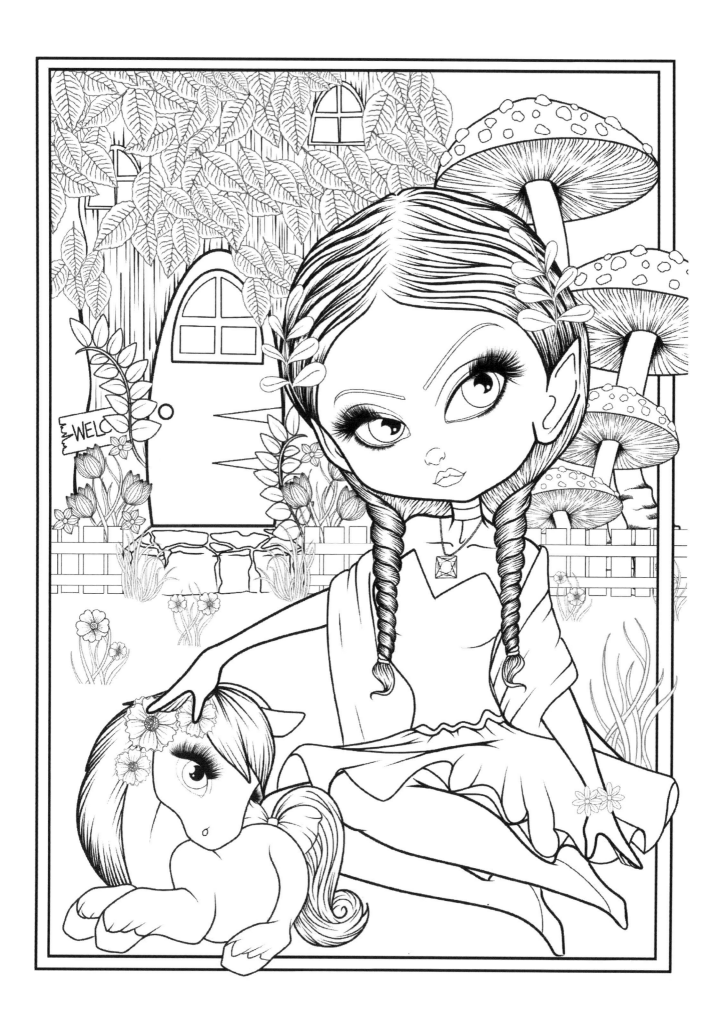

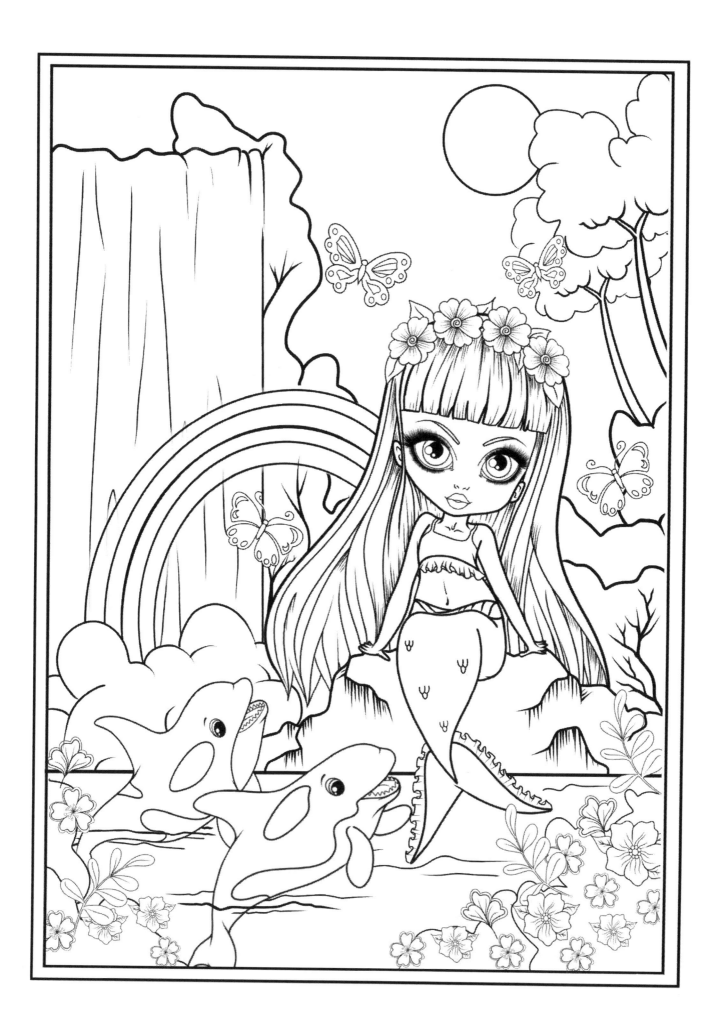

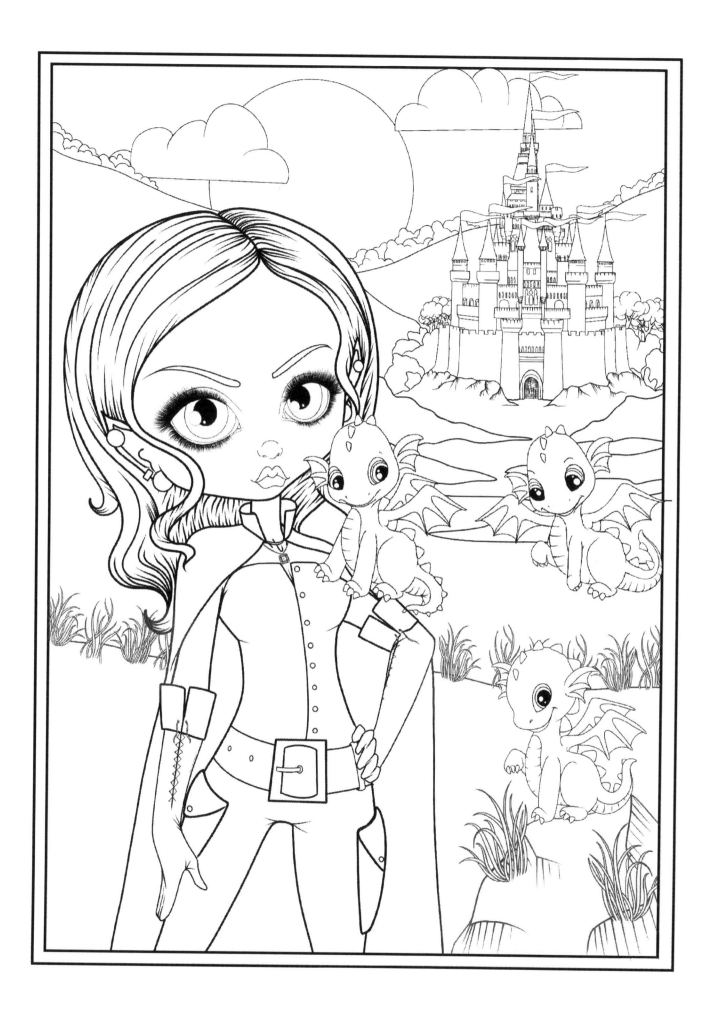

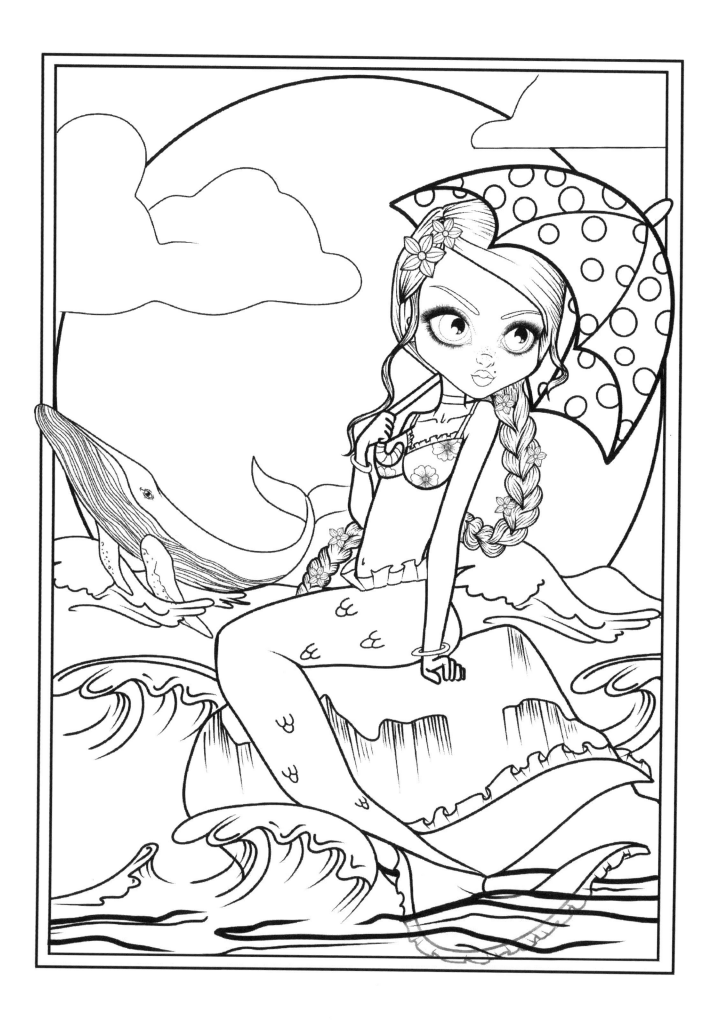

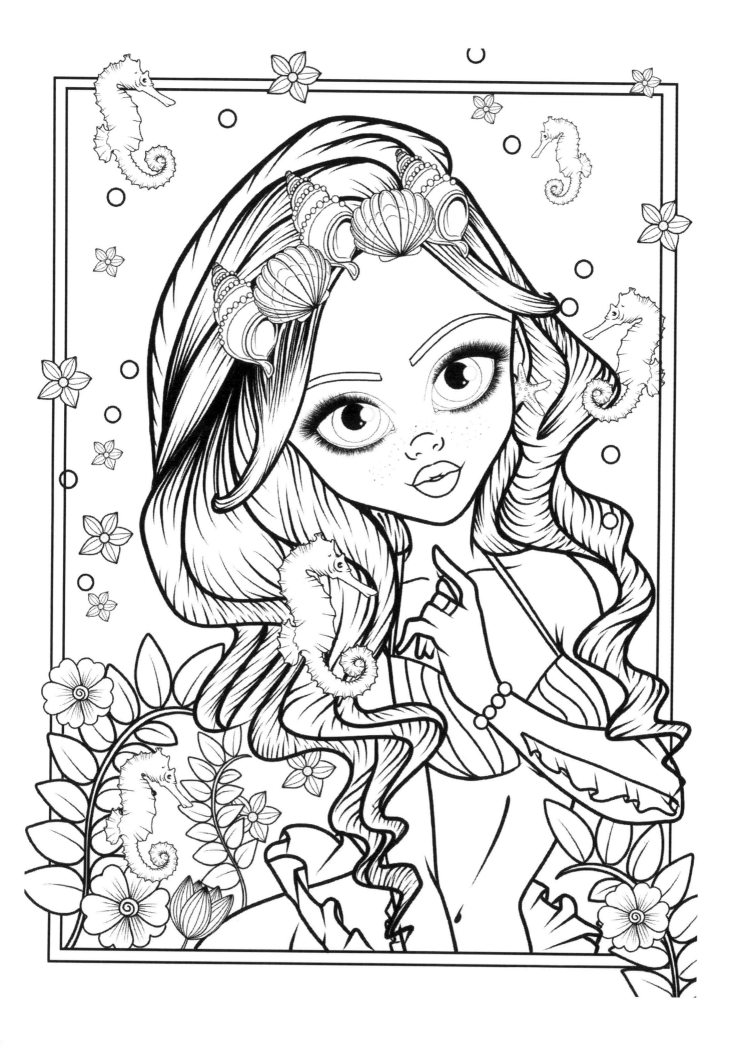

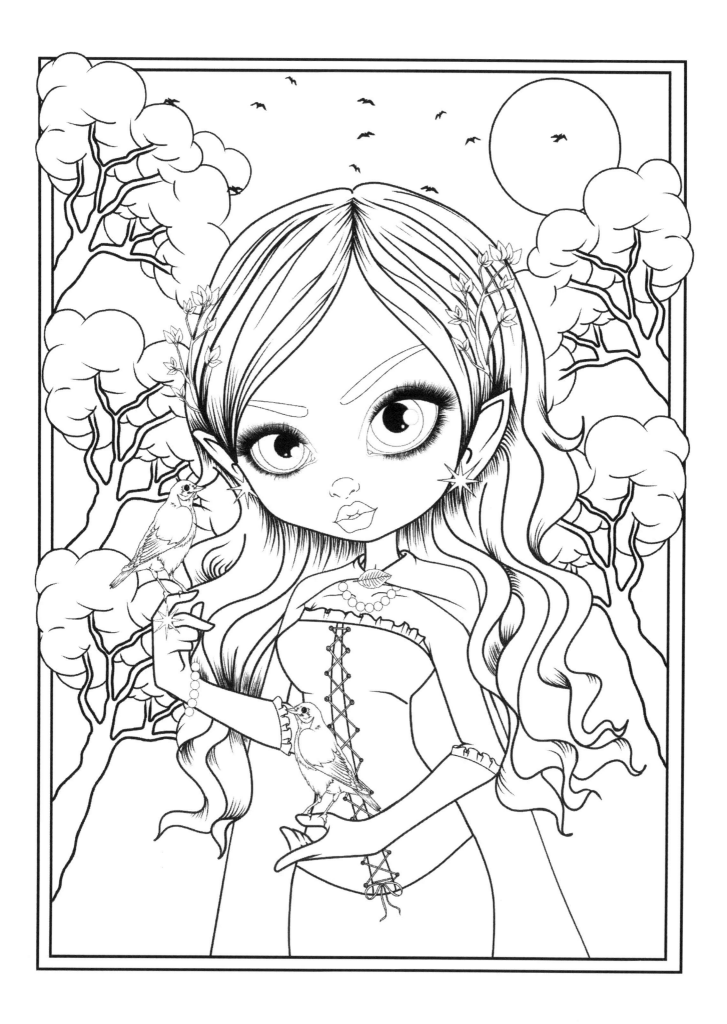

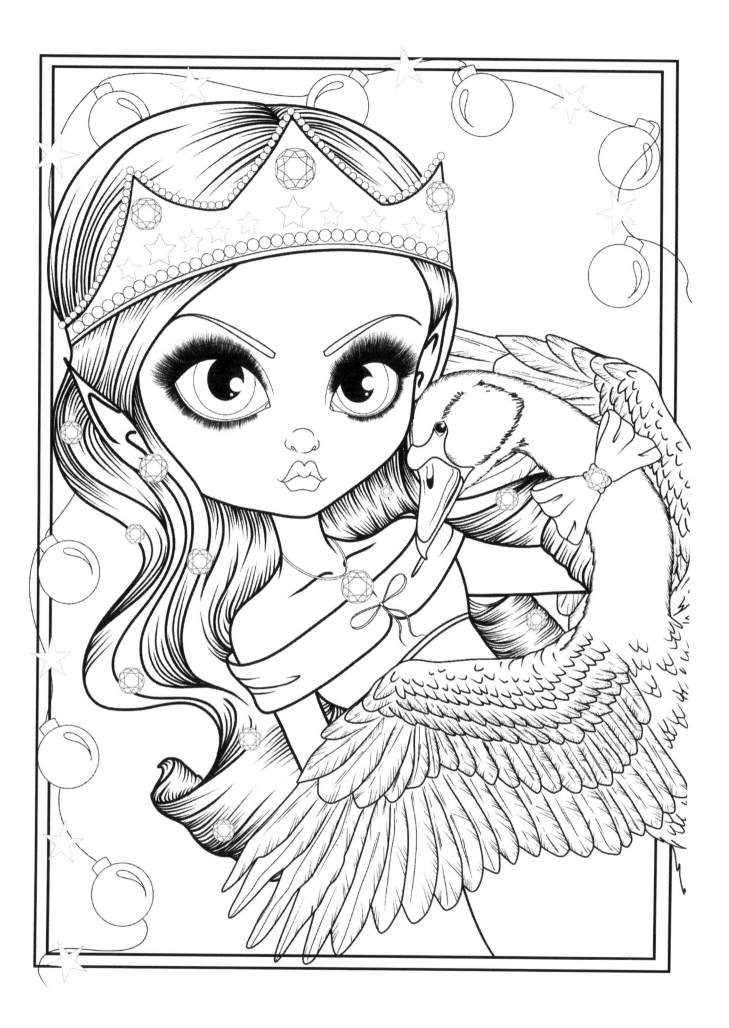

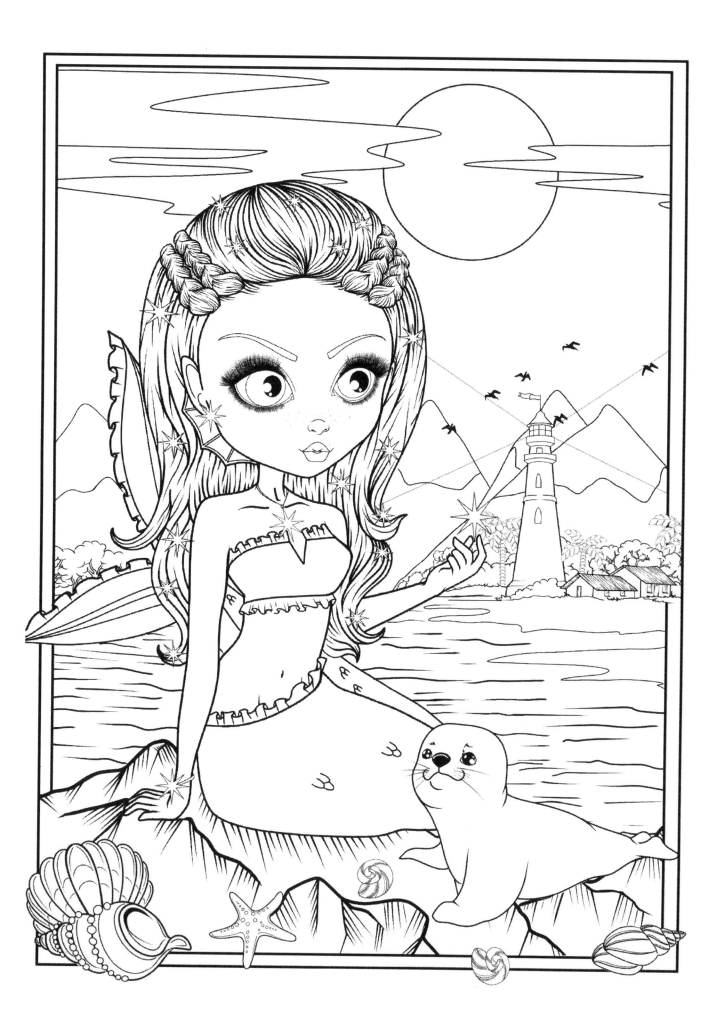

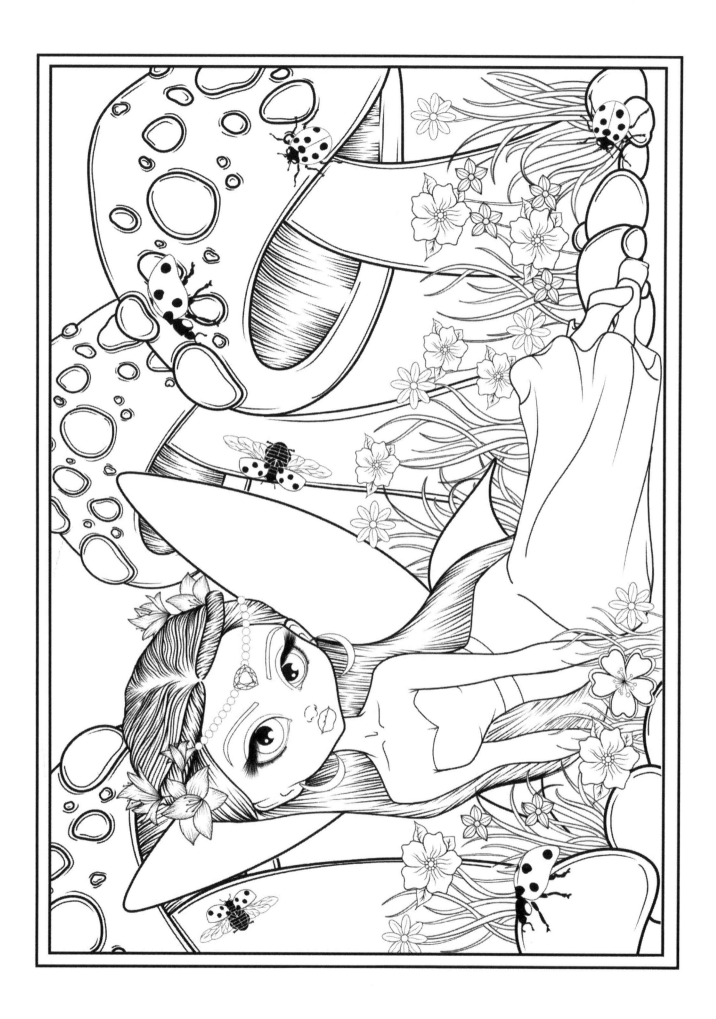

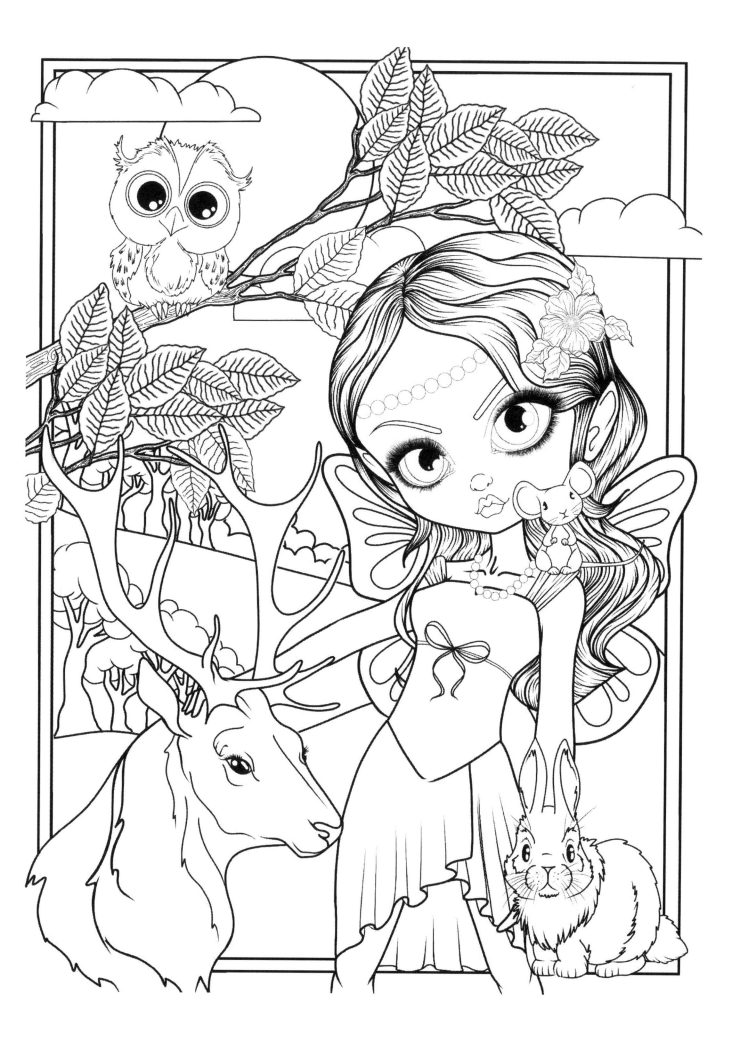

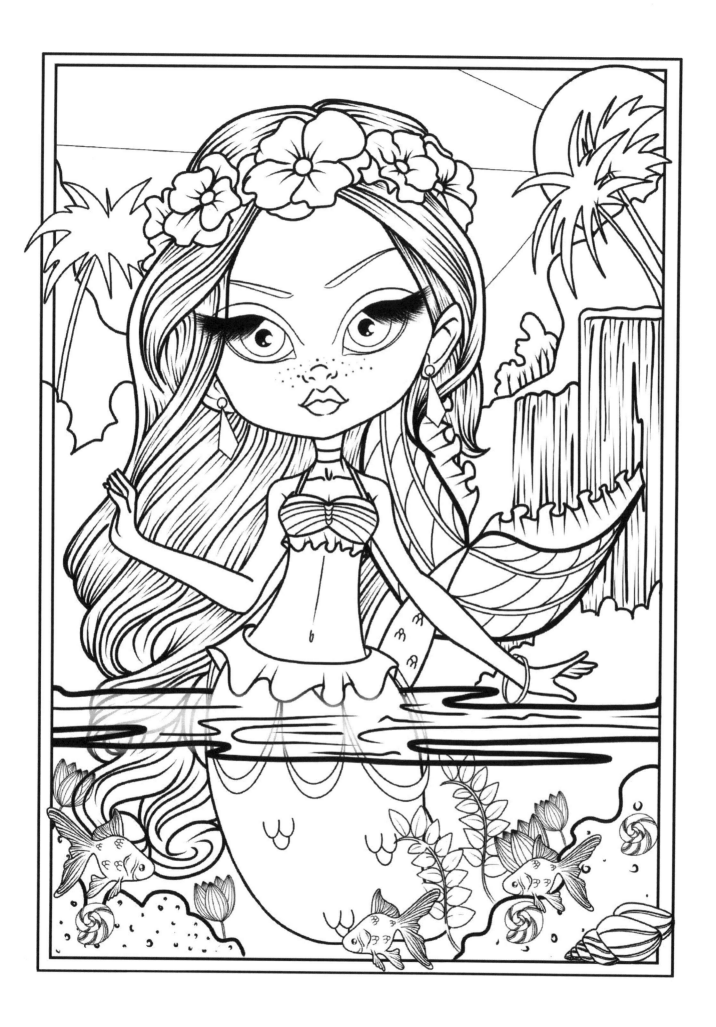

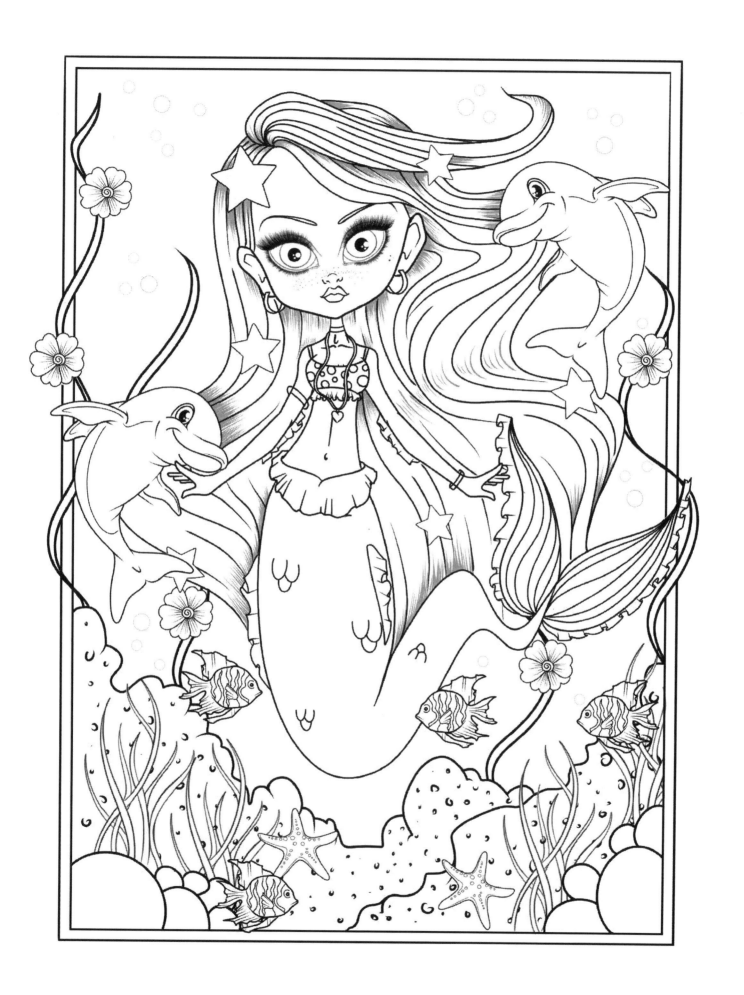

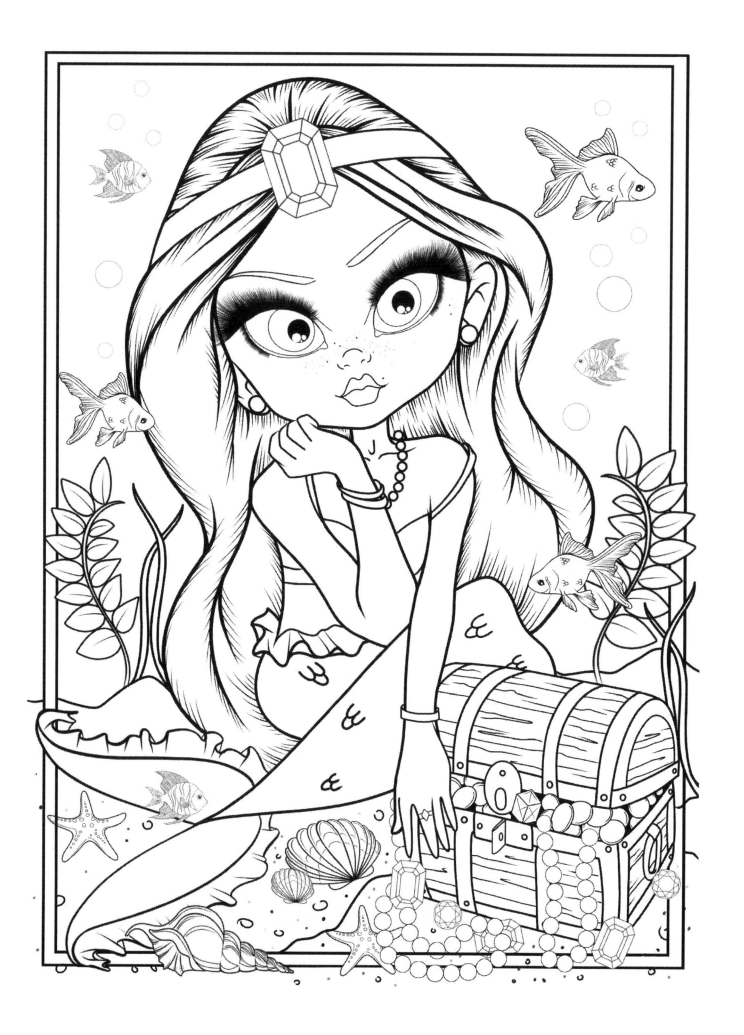

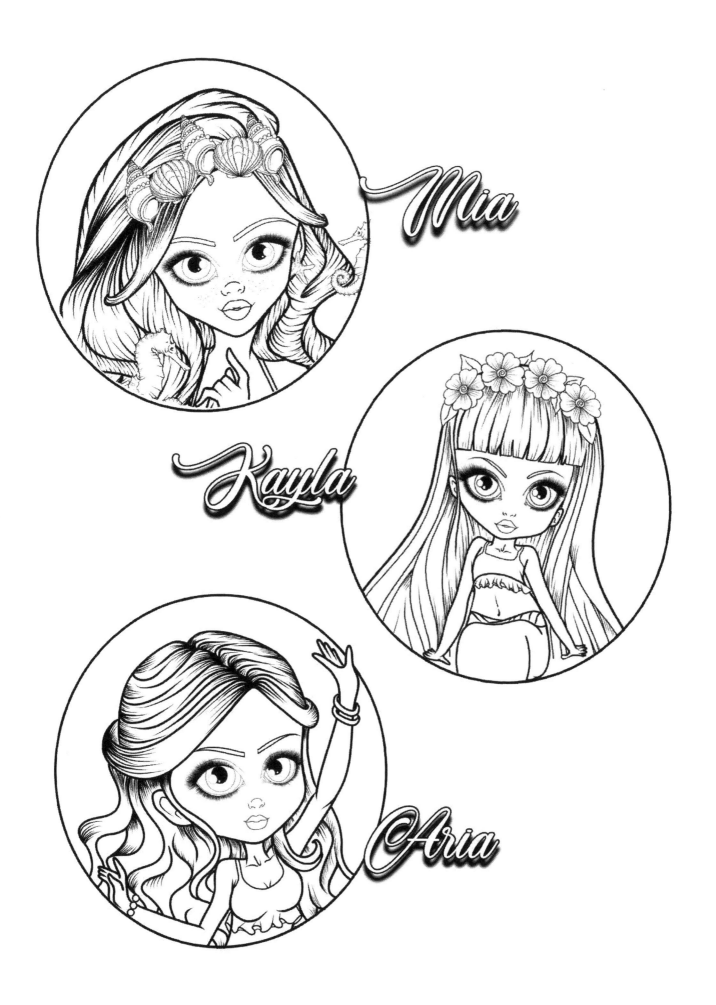

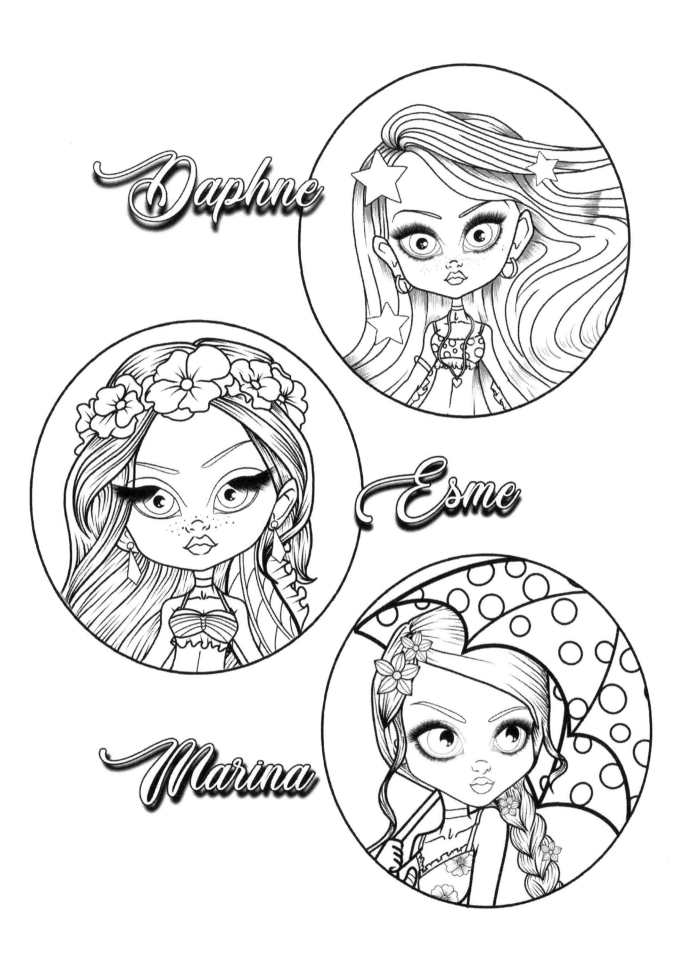

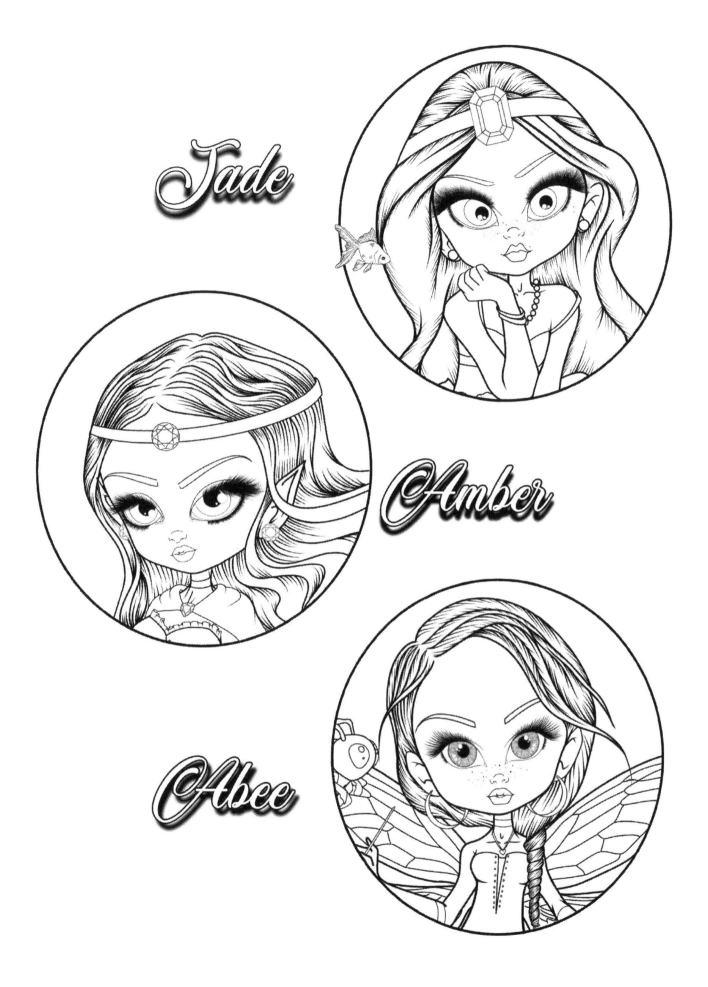

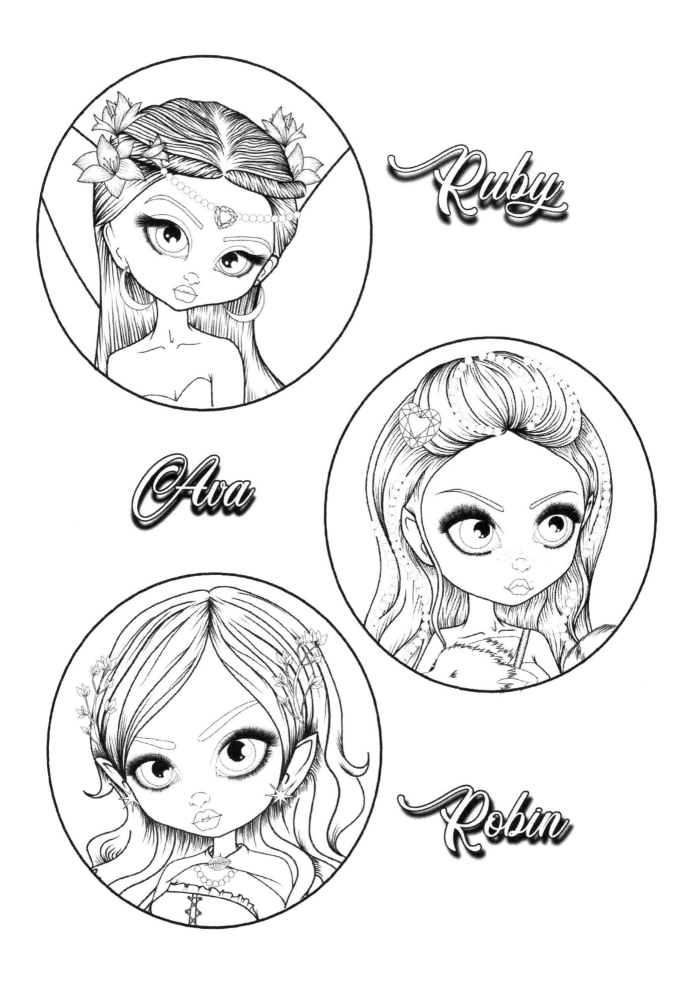

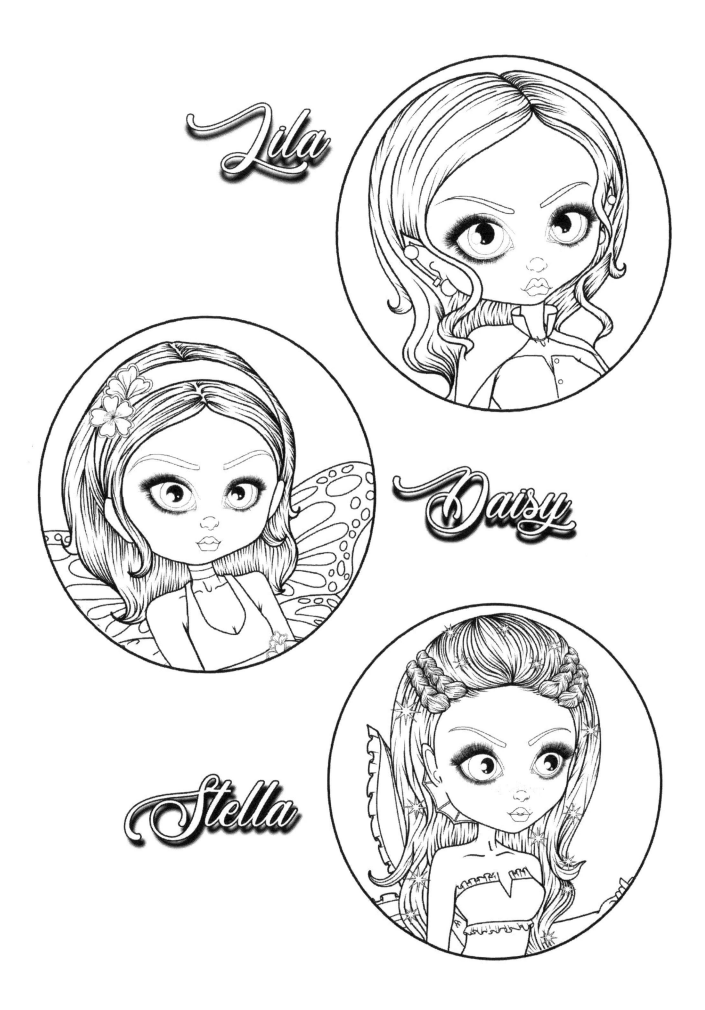

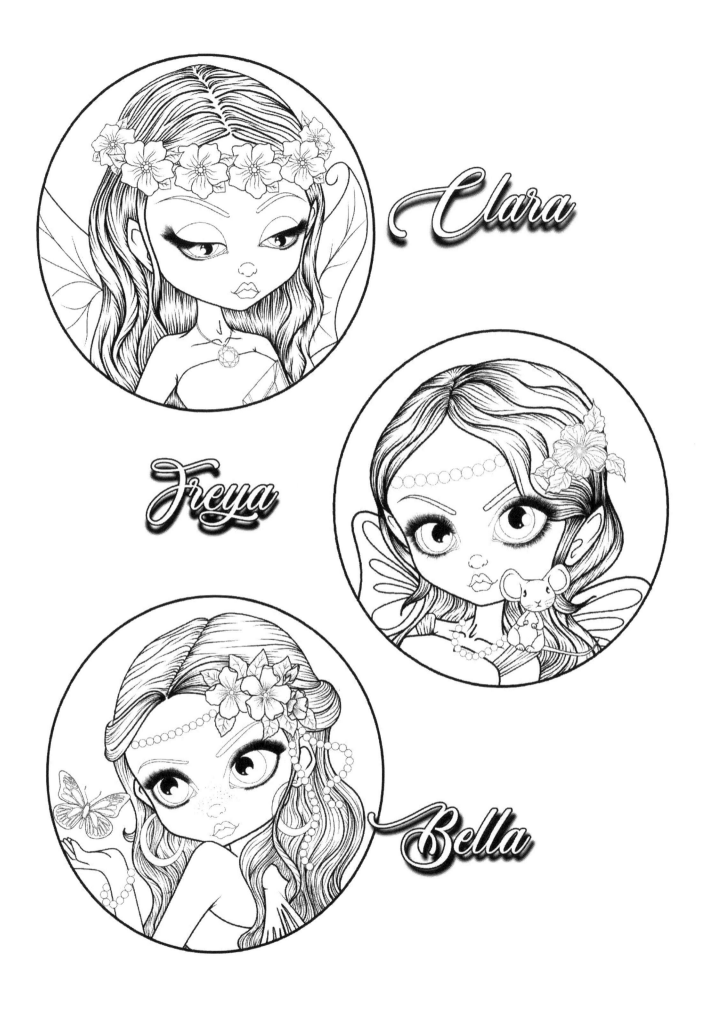

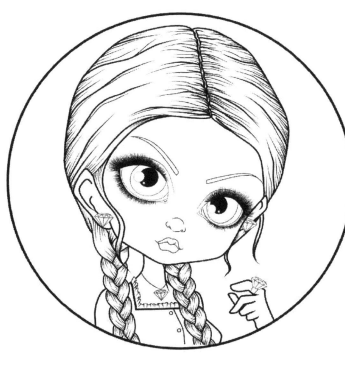
Bailey

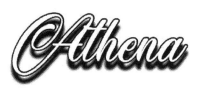
Athena

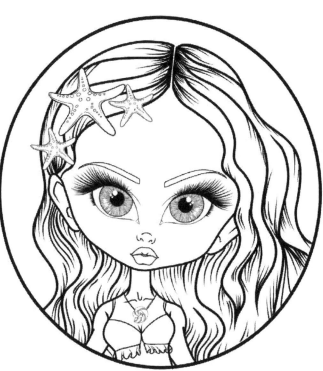

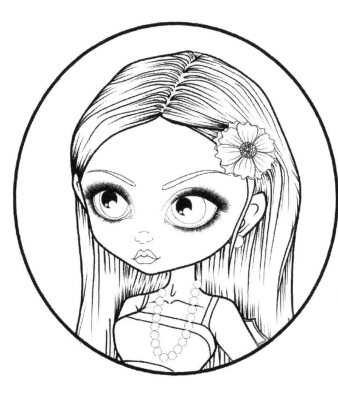
Amethyst

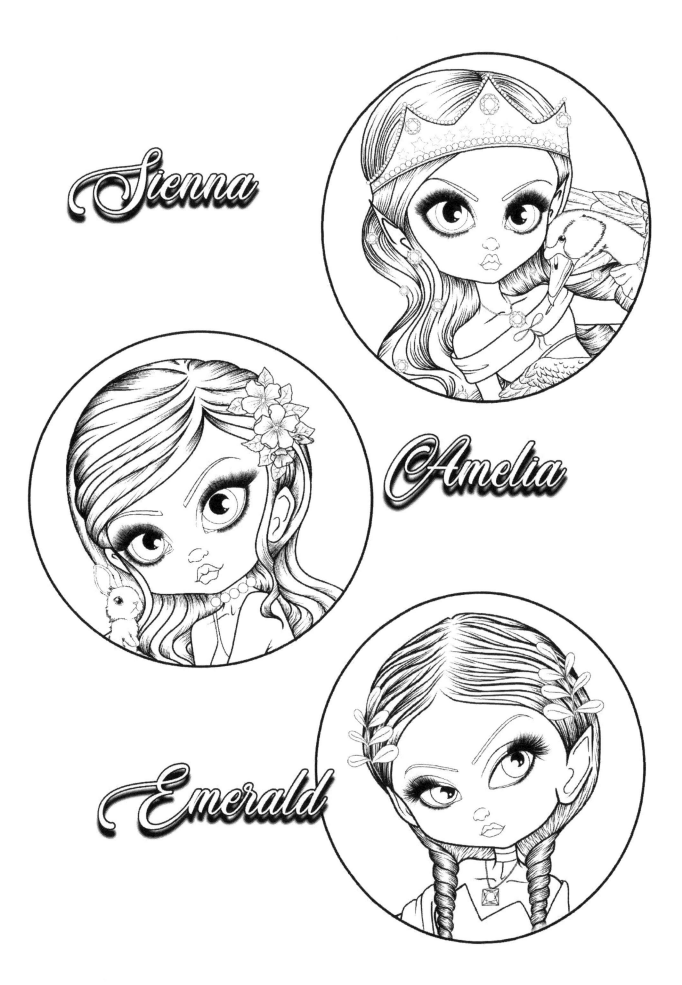

Skin tone Practise sheet

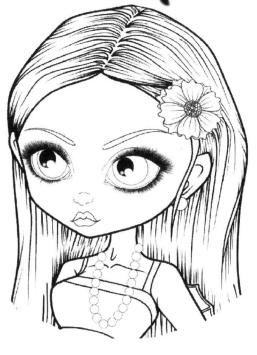
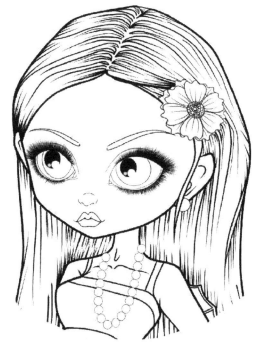
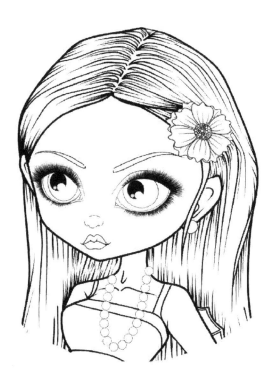
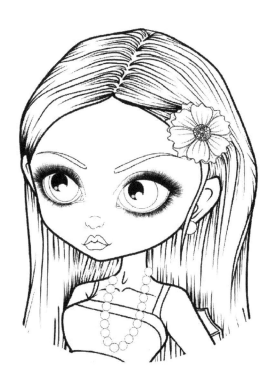

Skin tone Practise sheet

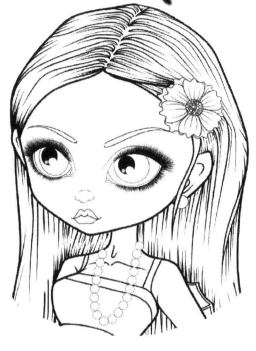
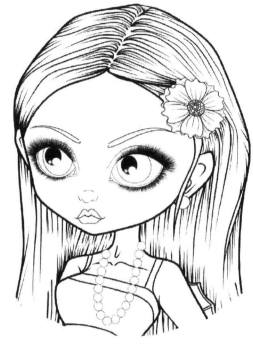
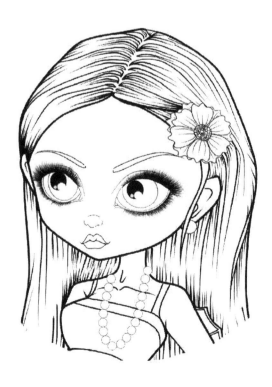
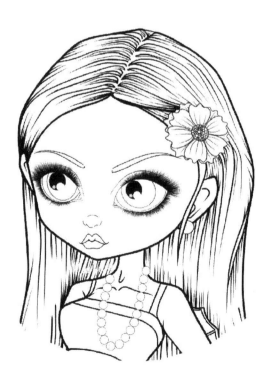

Colour swatch index

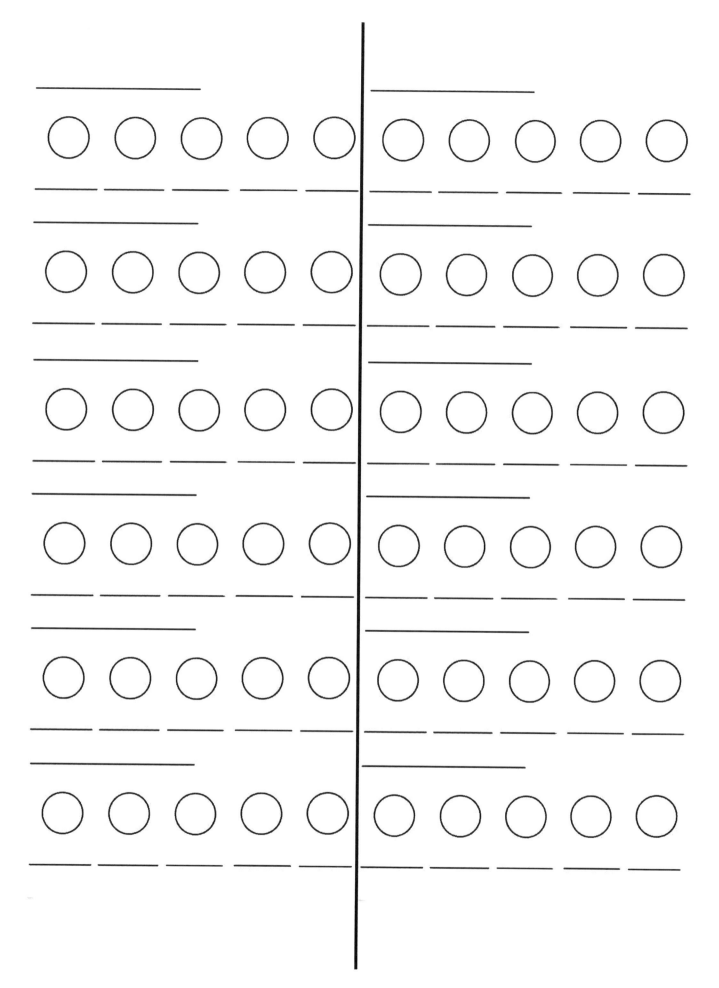

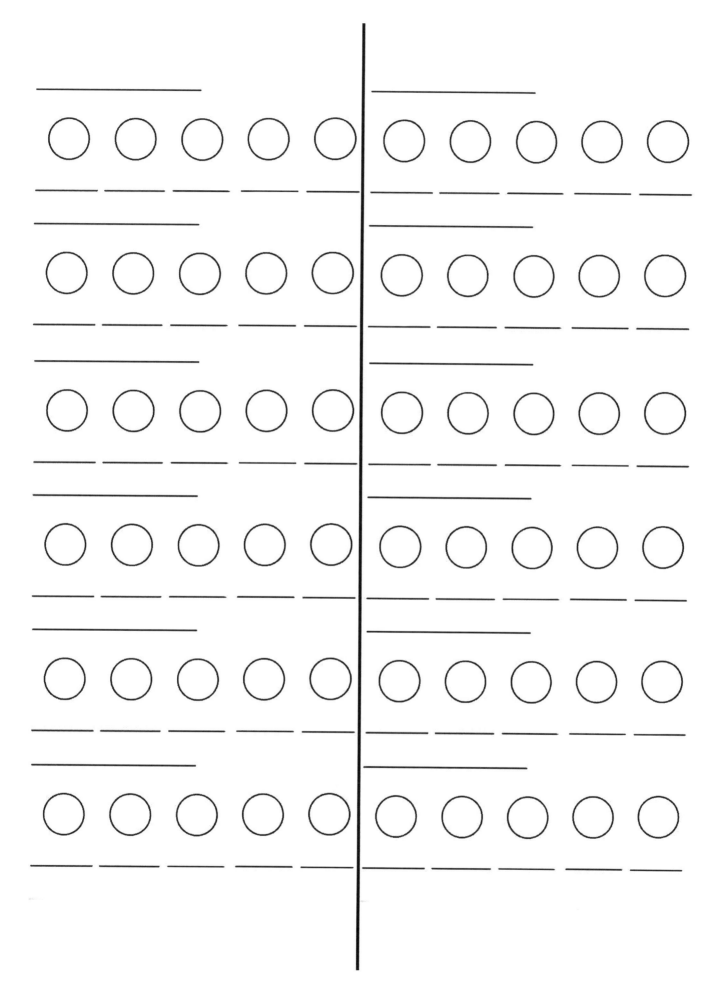

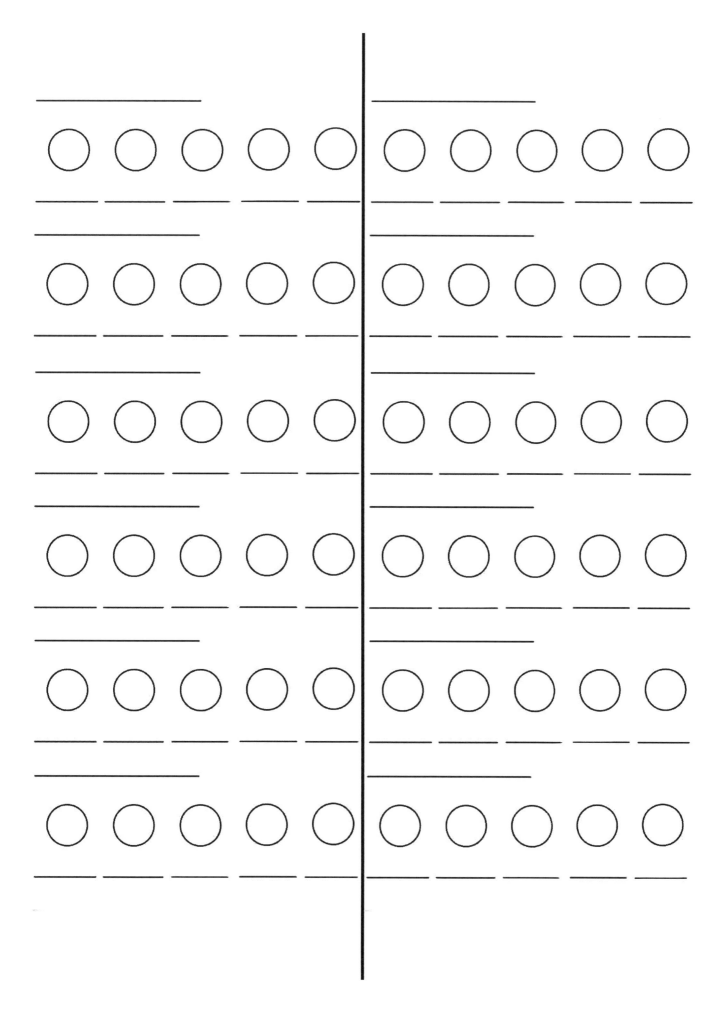

Made in the USA
Middletown, DE
25 July 2019